PAX

An Anthology of Southern Maryland Poetry

George Miller, *Editor* Elisavietta Ritchie, *Consulting Editor* Donald Grady Shomette, *Graphic Design* The Wineberry Press 2019

Copyright 2019 © by The Wineberry Press

All rights reserved, including the right to reproduce this book or portions thereof in any form or by any means, electronic or mechanical, including photocopying, recording, or by any information storage and retrieval system, without permission in writing from the publisher, PO Box 179, Friendship, Maryland 20758.

Book design by Donald Grady Shomette

Printed in the United States of America

FIRST EDITION

Library of Congress Cataloging-in-Publication Data

Pax: An Anthology of Southern Maryland Poetry. – 1st ed.

Includes poetry, photographs and illustrative matter

ISBN. 978-1-7332326-0-9.

1. Poetry. 2. Southern Maryland. 3. Hile, Doug; Jones, Rocky; Lassman, Kate; Lynn, Cliff; Miller, George; Ritchie, Elisavietta; Ritchie, Elspeth Cameron; Shelden, Suzanne; Shomette, Carol; Shomette, Donald Grady; Smallwood, Jeff; Webb, Laura Stewart; Van Wie, Joanne

TABLE OF CONTENTS

Author	Work	Page
Doug Hile	Used to be Spinnakers	22
	Blackie	26
Rocky Jones	In This Circle	14
	The History of Shit and Apple Butter	21
	Relics You Can Purchase From Me, Discreetly	36
Kate Lassman	Hope's Poem	6
	Seagull Song	32
Cliff Lynn	not spiderman	12
	rum and rainwater	19
	one/sixteenth man	34
George Miller	The Wreck of the Toni Marie	15
	Twenty-Minute Cliff	25
	The Crossing	30
	Sky Burial	33
Elisavietta Ritchie	Camille Pissarro's *Bather* Reminisces	8
	Sunset, December	18
	We Wake Beside an Invisible River	23
Elspeth Cameron Ritchie	Jewelweed	7
	Notes on the Death of a Deer	9
	Spring Lettuce	28
Suzanne Shelden	Riverside	16
	Audience	31
Carol Shomette	Zipline	13
	Last Flight	29
Donald Grady Shomette	Nightmare	11
	The Affair	17
	Lepidopterist	20
	The Graveyard of Ships	27
Jeff Smallwood	Final Stroke -	10
	Communion	24
	Drift	35
Laura Stewart Webb	Essential	2
	Some Gods	4
Joanne Van Wie	How to tell one man from another	3
	Nights	5

Essential

Not everyone sees the repeating face of a wolf
leaning in three times, a turned-down page
that might growl from underneath its corner

the whites of its eyes, its corduroy snout.
If you see it, today, for the first time,
it is essential not to panic.

Panic is for people who don't know that the wolf is there.

When you know that the wolf is there

everyday magic of Ireland still defines green;
so, too, emerald flash of grass at Malibu Creek State Park
love child of winter rains after scorching summer fire.

Blue means deep water reflecting open sky—
and a ward against the evil eye, a Stevie Wonder necklace
of matrixed turquoise worn by The Bride.

Daylily ribbons of sunshine explain yellow;
as does the alchemy-iris ablaze around a black hole's pupil
its steady gaze on us from light years away.

And no frame, however beautifully
it displays your advantages,
will ever contain you again.

Laura Stewart Webb

How to tell one man from another

Whether it is possible to fall silent.

Whether one whisper looks like another.
Whether there is a quiet staggering around
the openings or not. Whether
there are openings or whether
they are just crumb trails.

Whether the crumb trails lead,
whether you would starve
from the empty attached to the crumbs.
Whether you would listen.

Whether you would listen to your stomach.
Whether anyone with a stomach
would starve for your stomach.
Take a moment to imagine.
A handful of ripped hem, a handful of hair,
a handful.
What you hold lies under the curved lunula.
What you hold lies.

Whether you hold back parts in the after shadow:
the ran on rain, or burn on burnt.
Whether you hold out for that sell by date,
on truth.

How many layers you have to remove
before you can touch   the heart.
This, I think, is unnerving:
the shedding of once-careful surfaces,
the eventual exposure of one self after another.
It leads to the belief that what you touch can be
somehow distinguished.

Joanne Van Wie

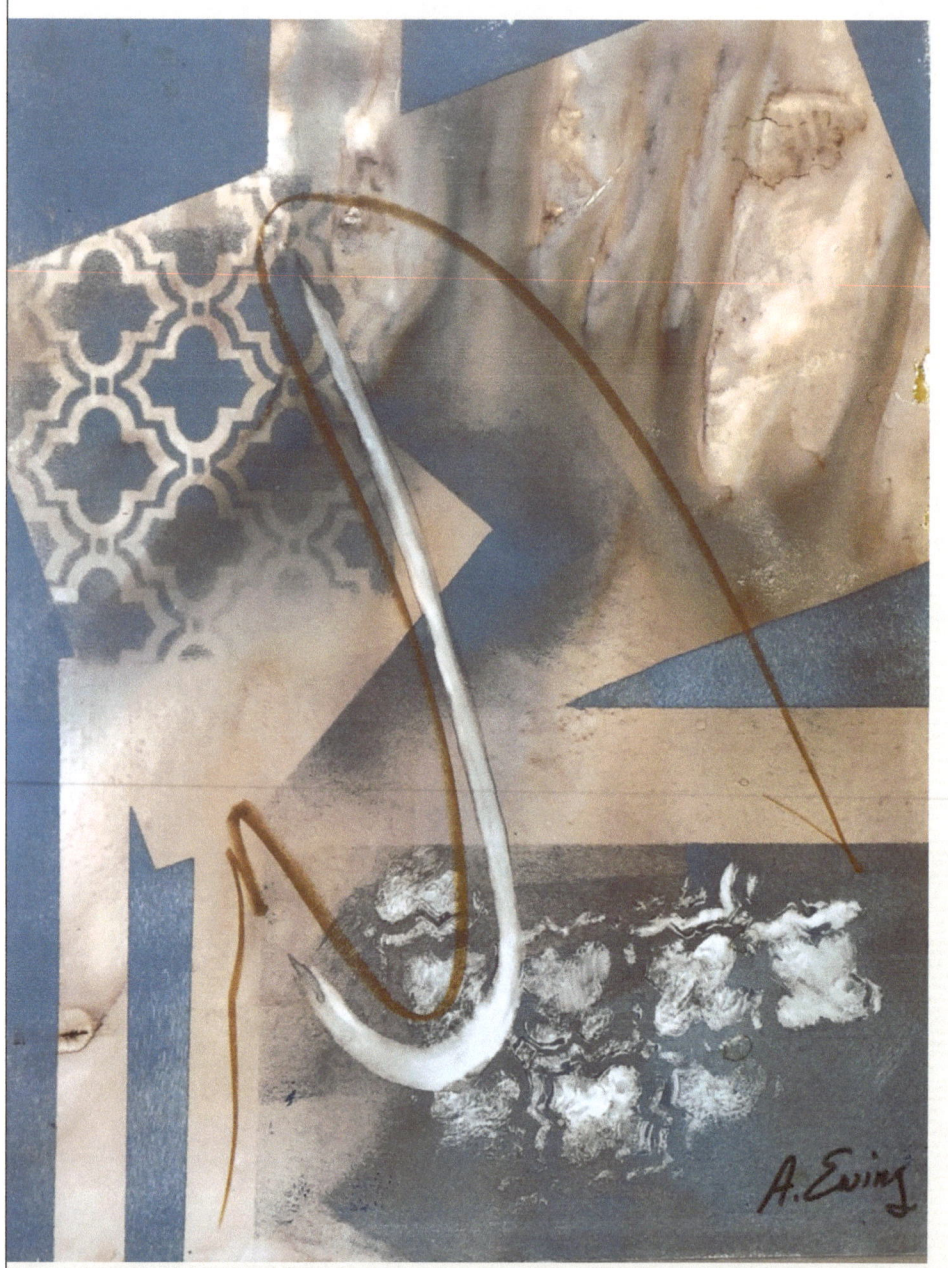

Some Gods

I never finished Karen Armstrong's
A History of God,

so I didn't know that anyone was wondering
if the gods had a future or might even have died.

During "The God of the Philosophers"
your hook of faith caught in my mouth;

since then I have been bleeding gold dust from my gums
dreaming in pink and white sprinkles

of how some gods

made a myth of us
to warm their own cold winter nights

rained cherry blossoms
down on your head and my upturned mouth

veiled our secrets
from their more Old Testament counterparts

read the most tender parts of our story
from behind a blue picture-book sky.

Laura Stewart Webb

Nights

Some nights have crescent moons
like the cup of your hand
or the spoon-edge of whispers.
& how the black sky remembers,
you held me a moment too long.
I wish nights would be without
the violence of promises & if
I were to see you again & everyone
we once opened had disappeared
I would bend down with you & rebuild
any protective walls that this earth
allowed us to give it –
because what is a night but an ongoing
darkness with hope of a phase change
taking place, & no claiming of
adjacent bodies can save us. The sun
rises always in the east & sets on itself
before we're done memorizing its voice.
& that dream, there, inside the cover
of your mind, how it dares to conjure
up past vows mid-spoken, as though
we would forget who lived there once
& when? As if we could forget that if
you open a wound & stop it with
someone else's soul, there will always
be an opening still, a partially filled
crescent edge cutting
the night sky.

Joanne Van Wie

Hope's Poem

I need a poem.
I've been looking all day,
but found none
at the grocery store,
among the bills I paid,
or in with the laundry.
No poems today
in the painting above my desk
or in all the music
I loaded on my phone.
No poems today.
Then Hope, the regal brown tabby,
jumps on my lap and purrs.
I have a poem.

Kate Lassman

Jewelweed

Hollow stems overstep my garden.
Weeds shade our begonias, lily bells.
Forgotten since their manic birth
pansies stretch weak stems,
velvet hearts arch toward shielded sun.

I yank out jewelweed.
Dirt embraces roots,
but resistance is weak.
The grass is tougher,
leaving foxholes where
a tattered mouse lies,
my cat's tribute abandoned.

This final weeding comes too soon.
I will be transplanted from summer
to the Cold War, Korea,
where tanks run down foreign flowers,
cooks serve dogs for lunch.

To pull up friendship is the hardest.
Some goodbyes are soft pops,
scars soothed by rain.
Leaf bags line time's curb.

Now my hoe catches on brambles.
Blackberry thorns
snag my heart as I leave,
and etch your name.

Elspeth Cameron Ritchie

Camille Pissarro's *Bather* Reminisces

I must have been beautiful back then,
am still surprised how many men pursued...

I let them think me but a starchy prude
until we paddled up the river when
the day was fair, light yellow, blue and green.

I was afraid the sun would leave
freckles on my breasts and we'd conceive
an unexpected child from where we'd been
cavorting in the shallows by the bank
of tiger lilies, peppermint and moss --

We yearned for more, but foliage was dank
with spilled champagne and sticky with cassis.

A need to pee, then nettle stings, kept me
from further loss of maidenhood...
Each loss is the first, and never quite the same.
Those early days, I never understood.

I have made many famous but forget their names,
dear artists who would sketch me in the nude...

I was a willing model: French plumbing then was crude
so they would scrub me till I shone, then came
to hang on these renown museum walls,
my loveliness immortalized in paint.

Although my grandmothers would faint,
I have no regrets I gave to art my all.

Elisavietta Ritchie

Notes on the Death of a Deer

Elspeth Cameron Ritchie

Swans roost on laps of waves,
yell at sun and terns.
We spill onto February's beach.
Two gifts: a thaw,
and my new love is here.
Snowdrops bob through brown leaves.
Green wheat sweeps the field.
Ospreys dive in shafts of wind.

But, a duck blind sprouts horns
between unbeaten poles and juniper.
A flock of painted duck
decoys rides the waves.

Local men hunt, grow tobacco,
scrape oysters from hard beds.
In the city, we have rank,
here, only orange vests
shield us from country fire.

I shout, my love stumbles.
Do hunters aim
at our muscled hearts?
Buzzards flap and rise.
He steps onto the carcass
of a stag tethered by sand.

A fresh kill, swarmed by sandflies.
One antler with eight points
aloft, the other horn,
under ground oyster shells.

Was he killed here, or, bleeding, parched,
straggle to the river to die?

His eye, fixed, shrouds his killing.
No boats behind the blind.
Red-winged blackbirds claim reeds.
Swans, heedless, bob on.
Murder guts my throat.
My fingers twitch, wish
for a trigger to return rage.

That buck led his does
through holly and cedar
to raid butter winter lettuce.
I watched him through my window
as, sleepless, I wrestled
with my husband's betrayal.
My son called him "Rudolph."

I'd hoped this farm was sacred,
shielded by posted signs.
How do other mothers feel
when their children are shot?

I do not cry as we leave,
it's only a goddamned deer.

My black cat was run over
when I was twelve.
She slept on my bed,
protected me. I'm grown,
there is no safety left.

Final Stroke

Off-trail in a thicket of green
Where the stick-tights adhere to my socks
And cockleburs hitchhike unseen
I paused on my wandering walk

Abandoned here deep in the trees
Its roof full of craters and gaps
An old livestock barn no one sees
With walls on the verge of collapse

The stalls are all quiet and bare
Mud floors with a scent of decay
Yet one has a table and chair
And a cork board with frame torn astray

But the one thing I found most bizarre
A typewriter placed there in the center
As if someone sat writing memoirs
Embracing the dirt and the weather

Platen without paper, ribbon so old
The chair lined up straight, ready to type
Keys full of dust with a carriage of mold
I wonder, what was its last letter like

Was an arm of **e** the last one to strike
With warmth of 'love' or chill of 'goodbye'
Maybe dark tones of 'hate' or 'dislike'
Or a painful closing with tears in the 'eye'

Perhaps it was **n** in 'unknown'
Or a resigned 'disappointment' of **t**
Maybe the 'chill' of an **l** to the bone
Or the sly silent **s** of 'chablis'

I've since made my way home from the wild
But the mystery continues to flourish
I've thought of it often and smiled
That secretive home in the forest

I like to think its last strike of a key
Carried by breeze and the song of the lark
Was neither an **r** nor an **i** nor a **b**
But a lingering brave question mark

Jeff Smallwood

Nightmare

A little rubber creature
    no smaller than my fist
with pumpkin colored eyes
    and purple skin cysts
hovered over my face
    displaying a blistered complexion
feigning innocence of evil
    to avoid my detection.
Its gargoyle-like tongue
    lolled about lips putrid yellow
mucous drooling aplenty
    over my pristine white pillow.
We stared at each other
    through moonless night gloom
passing hours on end
    in my tiny bedroom.
I watched through slit lids
    faking sleep through the night
as it surveilled my every move
    to prevent my sudden flight.
At witching hour it blinked
    still watching and waiting
now licking and clicking
    its mouth salivating.
"Is he awake?" said the creature
    standing on all six feet.
"Is he alive? My heavens.
    I need something to eat."

Suddenly it lunged
    curled lips gripping my nose.
with its long rubbery tongue
    a serrated hose.
Then twisting about,
    all slobber and grip,
it vanished into darkness
    like the snap of a whip.
As it faded from view
    with my nose in its maw
my snout and snot gone
    I lay there in awe.
Where proboscis once stood proud
    Roman, equine, cocksure
the space once adorned
    now just a puncture.
My pillow is sticky
    I daren't move from my bed
for the nightmare still hovered
    somewhere in my head.
Then came dawn's light
    through my window it burned
with the miracle of day
    my nose had returned.

Donald Grady Shomette

not spiderman

Cliff Lynn

ol' patrick parker's end began at 13, rejected
by colleen before a first kiss, rejected by susan
after just one kiss. a tragic poet, moved sprinklers

through the hay after dark, always after dark. last
time I saw ol' pat parker his skin was colorless
'cept for the angry sores on his hands, and his face

was a broken clock. his eyes were nervous marbles,
but those were his eyes even before gin and poetry.
he blamed his parents for not calling him peter, if

they'd only called him peter, he would've grown
up spiderman. instead they slung *patrick* 'round his
scrawny baby neck, and he grew up, well, like he had

grew up, pushing middle age and still hamstrung
by his non-superhero name.   nobody I know saw
nary an obituary nor a death certificate, so ol' pat

parker's cause of passing passes as a mystery to all.
some say cancer of the liver-stomach-kidney, but me
I suspect ol' pat parker just got tired of bein' ol'

pat parker. the girls (we still call 'em that, even
though today they're north of fifty), say it's from
a broken heart. I say man that's 37 years of dyin'.

then we all just sit shutmouthed, studyin' the hay
as it slowly slides to seed.

Zipline

On the lam from the cold-blooded caress
Of winter's arctic grasp,
I catapult myself into an equatorial elusion
Under a cerulean ceiling
Above verdant hues beyond crayola dreams.

Forsaking reason for a chance thrill,
I trust a gossamer spider thread
To hurtle past fleeting vistas of emerald ripples,
Witnessed by somnolent three-toed gymnasts and
Saurian sun-god worshippers.

Tearing between roosts in this surreal canopy,
My icy lover's tentacles disappear.
Each sound barrier breaking launch brings
Howls and screams of a simian song,
Echoed in my own unrestrainable aria.

Fast forward a fortnight,
Skip latitudes to be glacially consumed again.
Bony fingers of my barren woodland canopy
Stretch to an azure overhead,
Waiting to be unfrozen from suspended animation.

Subtle sepia and sienna allow surprise glimpses
Of defiant steadfast evergreens,
Holly and Christmas fern in holiday denial.
Unseen silent eyes await the vernal rebirth
To briefly impersonate my tropic tryst.

Carol Shomette

Rocky Jones

In This Circle

I shall draw a great circle to summon you.
Within the circle, I shall place
 • a lock of hair from the legendary Shirley Temple
 • a tiger's claw
    given to me by an antique dealer
       so it's okay because
          I mean
             antiques are old,
             and this one,
             given, not sold,
             so, I'm not supporting
             a *new* tiger-claw market,
 • and a counterfeit
garment thread
said to have been worn by
Sir Isaac Newton
but totally not —

Within this circle, I shall affix a speaker
and a music player
and let into this sacred space
a carefully-selected group of songs
by the Partridge Family —

And, I haven't really worked this out yet, but,
I'll set up some sort of way to diffuse the scent
of Boston Baked Beans candy.

If my magic circle
does not bring you to me,
I shall beseech
Congress,
and rich people,
and the Ascended Christ,
that they might team up
and,
either speak on my behalf,
or find some other way
to salve
my
poor,
moaning
heart.

The Wreck of the Toni Marie

You, my flesh, my son, alone on the boat
when the wind shifted.

A squall from the west, a cold dark cloud
between you and the shore.

A rookie mistake: the jib, the head sail,
you approached the wind too sharply.

This I taught you over and over
when we sailed together in fiercer winds:
    Reef the sail, pull leeward,
    downward, slowly uncoil, unfurl,
    head slightly into the wind,
    slacken the jib.

You in the storm, my son, alone
on the deck when the winds rose.

You lost our boat,
I lost my son.

George Miller

Riverside

Sheets of rain lift
up from the water
shimmering bright
where the sun can touch.

Curtains of gray
sweep into darkness
leaving behind
the wet bending reeds.

Suzanne Shelden

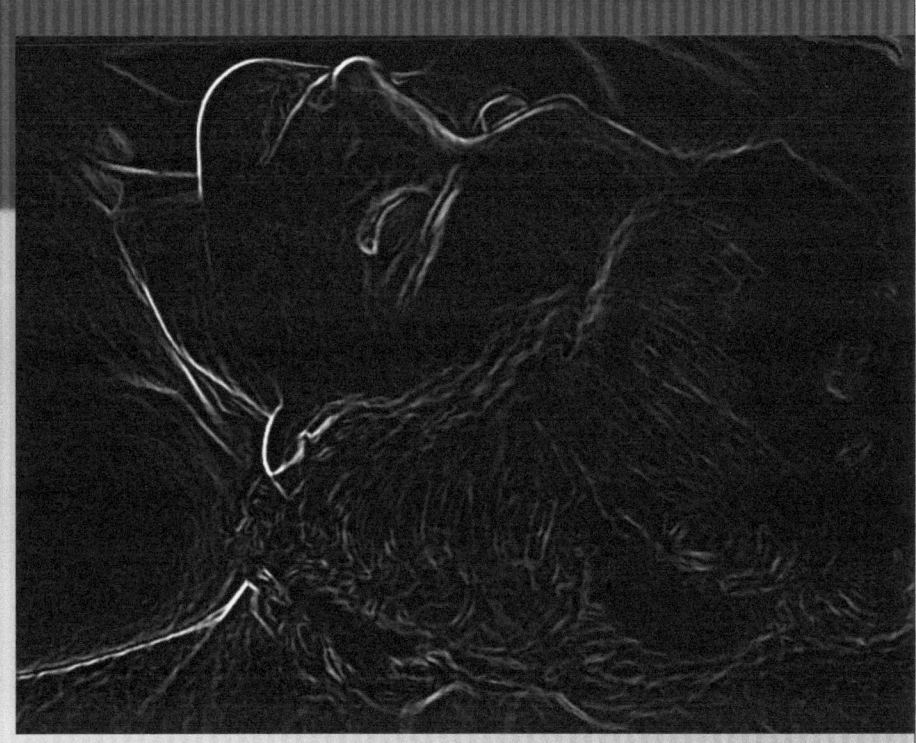

Your body lay on the bed
sweating of rut
never expended
a life unfulfilled
tangled with mine
again and again
forever
and never
senses eroding
and forgotten duties
gathering dust
as time disappears
in gushing wavelets of lust
in a corner somewhere
family and friends
we no longer miss
as the hours trickle by
since that last kiss.

THE AFFAIR

Again and again
no future no past
illusions of years
stretch endlessly before us
but never beyond
couplings of mere love.
We breathe heavily,
fearful of hesitation
for the loss that may ensue,
in a missed second of elation
again and again
in heedless copulation.
Again and again
we forget everything
we that can never be
and never complete.
My strength ebbs
with each encounter
but our flower is sweetened
again and again
until we blossom
and wither.
                Again.
                and
                again

Donald Grady Shomette

Sunset, December

Suddenly
celestial hounds bay -
hundreds of geese
in ragged patterns
above this autumnal terrain

One
flies
ahead
draws
the
chain
of
ganders
across
orange
sounds

Elisavietta Ritchie

rum and rainwater

a boy-o, he desires nothin' greater
than to set sail 'neath my ensign most black
wear the salt wind on his tanned hairless back
to eat stale hardtack and cold pepper bacon
drink rum and rainwater for breakfast

a boy-o, that he would not be tethered
by mothers, by man-made laws nor by borders
feel of cold steel in his boy-o hands be in order
ain't like murder, lads, if the buggers got it comin'!
then—rum and rainwater for breakfast

a boy-o, he covets *treasure island*'s treasure
dreams of digged-up iron trunks spilling over
with rubies, doubloons and ropes of pure silver
ripped from the velveter clutches of dyin' gentlemen
dreams of rum and rainwater for breakfast

a boy-o, he's the most impatient of blighters
can't wait to lose an arm, some toes or an eye
or be run right through in the meat of his thigh
to bathe in warm blood, aye, again, and again
to drink rum and rainwater for breakfast

Cliff Lynn

LEPIDOPTERIST

Butterfly with sails distended

Why, lovely thing, must your flight be ended?

Now my profession, that master of me

Must come to the fore and capture thee.

Those golden soft scales on wings dare not I mar

For now you must perish inside my jar.

Donald Grady Shomette

Rocky Jones

The History of Shit and Apple Butter

The differences between shit and apple butter are many and diverse.
"Shit" comes from the Latin, *shitulum*, which means poop.
Its bronzy sheen acts as a brain-trigger, telling us to "keep away!"
The brain processes this signal as a smell.

"Apple butter" comes from the French, *abletteur*, meaning poop.
Its bronzy sheen comes from the French as well.

Aristotle referred to shit and apple butter as the *quarreling twins*,
each insulting the other's physicality, neither accepting their similarity,
which is obvious to onlookers.

Only the wise onlooker, though, knows the true distinction.

Used to be Spinnakers

Now it's Sunset Cove.
A slow Sunday afternoon at home, so felt the need to revisit.
Hardly anyone there. Took a seat at the bar.
Bartender was busy with a group in the Big Room.

We had good times there, nice dinners, Sunday brunch...
They fixed your bourbon salmon the way you liked it, and your sweet potato.
Different now, pizza, burgers, appetizers. I ordered crab balls and a beer.
Ok but not Spinnakers. some crab, some dough, sauce helped.

A couple at the bar.
He was ... typical.
Short cargo pants, t-shirt, ball cap, five day facial growth,
she was affable, pleasant enough,
another couple came in later to meet them.
I did not engage or desire ... conversation.

Beach volley ball on the tv ... ESPN ...
someone's alma mater vs. someone elses'.
Low volume on muzak, but caught my attention.
Green Grass and High Tides.
I made a remark to the bartender who wasn't familiar with the song.
I said it was The Outlaws, better than Skynerds' Free Bird.

He didn't know either one,
said they play some strange stuff ... occasionally.
Sad. Forgotten history.

Realizing it was a mistake to come here.
Nothing stays the same.
I paid the check, tipped him ten bucks anyway.
On the way out, he introduced himself as Jason ...
said please come back soon.

I'll be back when they bring back bourbon salmon.

Doug Hile

We Wake Beside an Invisible River

Fog swishes through pines
screens our world inside a Japanese dawn,
veils deer among flowering quince.

Through the scrim of mists
we see the Buddha at Kamakura,
small deer we fed at Nara,

Cormorants with rings
around their throats bringing fish
to skiffs in the Inland Sea.

Mists melt, we see Fujiyama
surrounded by sapphire waves
and crowned with perpetual snows—

The tardy sun burns this day clear
over our gray-green cove.
Tide is covering marshes and sand.

Our great blue heron proclaims longevity
as he overflies cattails and huge pink
marshmallow flowers edging the cove.

The cormorant only passing through dives
for minnows, swallows them down his long neck
then, perched on a piling, airs his long narrow wings...

Far river banks are fringed with bent oaks
between fields of soybeans and pastures where
ebony steers graze beside our briny Patuxent...

One crane flies against the misty red sun
over a rice padi, pink petals, skinny reeds,
on an antique scroll on our Maryland wall.

Elisavietta Ritchie

Communion

In dew laden grass and predawn grey
a bovine inhabitant welcomes me in trespass
like a fresh brewed cup of earthy morning joe

Speckled pink nose of silky wet textured skin
in a sea of whiskers
my inner Attenborough narrates
enticing me to reach out and scratch my host on the chin

His Sherlockian tongue greets me through barbed wire
like an alien handshake
in search of an autumn apple or maybe a
generous portion of pumpkin flesh

Apologies my curious calf
I disappoint us both for I only have
roadside briers and conversation to offer

This gentile detective wanders off
case closed, reminding me who truly
had this morning's priorities in order

Returning to the campfire
I stir creamer into a second cup
with grass stained hands
and smile

Jeff Smallwood

Twenty-Minute Cliff

We met on the trails beneath the rock face,
she foraged for mushrooms in the underbrush,
I was lost, searching for the clearing
where I'd stowed my car.

She stumbled down the gully, grabbed my hand for balance,
"My name's Elsa. It's Dutch, short for Lijsbeth."

"Mushrooms," she rattled off the names:
"Hen of the woods, morels, shaggy manes."
She plucked them one by one.

"You'd best be on your way," she said.
"Twenty minutes after the sun sets
beyond the granite cliff, night, pitch black.
Let's find your car and get you out of here."

Blue eyes, alive, sparkling, a mind within, an intellect,
but mottled skin, blotches on her face and forearms.
I didn't ask. She offered when I stared.
"Too much time on the peaks above the clouds
where the sun beats down."

Years later our paths crossed again,
same trails, same mushrooms,
another lost car.

Now dark patches on her skin,
"Tumors," she explained.
"Sunlight takes its toll,
I don't have long."

Elsa knew sunset on the Blue Ridge,
twenty minutes, then pitch black.

George Miller

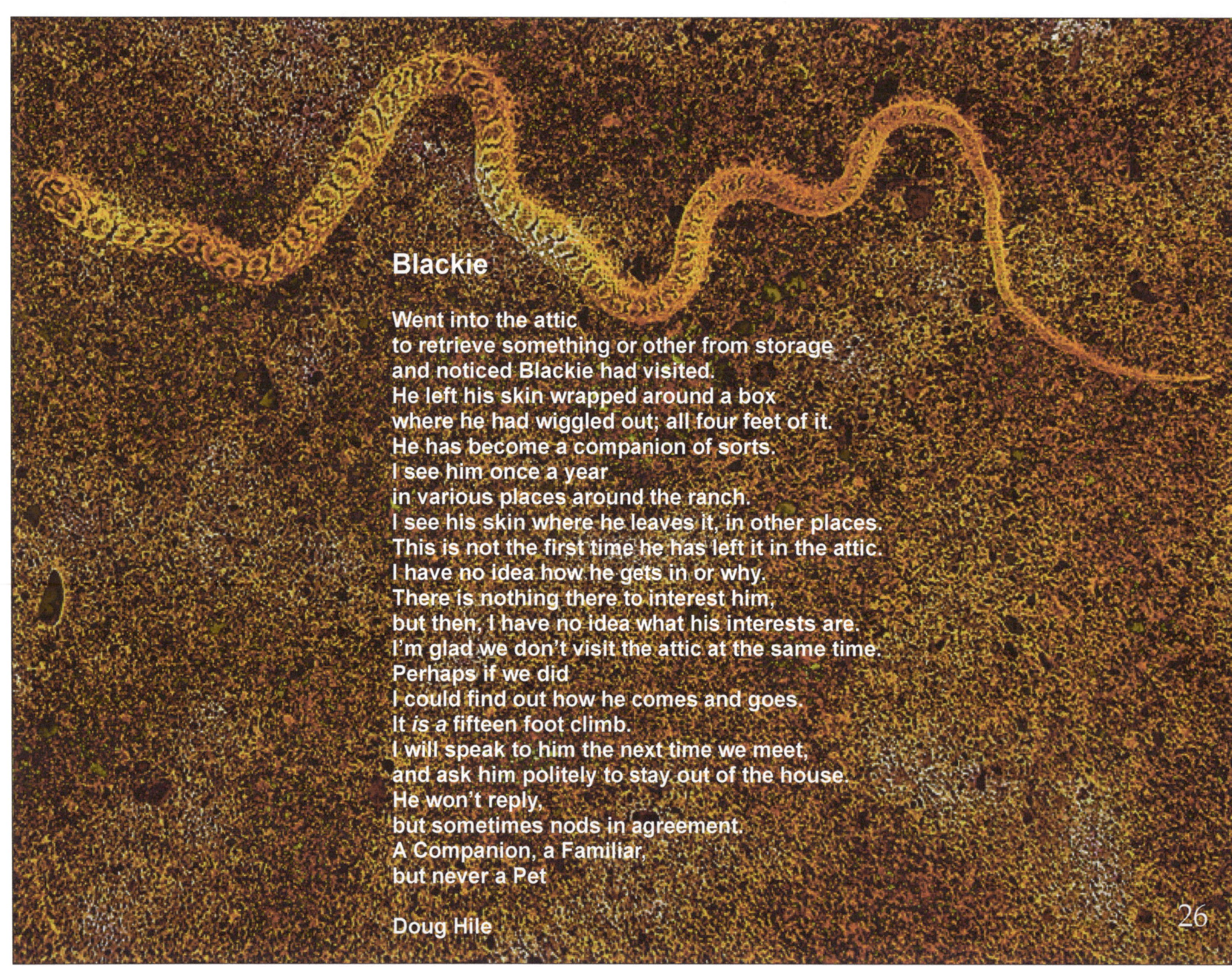

Blackie

Went into the attic
to retrieve something or other from storage
and noticed Blackie had visited.
He left his skin wrapped around a box
where he had wiggled out; all four feet of it.
He has become a companion of sorts.
I see him once a year
in various places around the ranch.
I see his skin where he leaves it, in other places.
This is not the first time he has left it in the attic.
I have no idea how he gets in or why.
There is nothing there to interest him,
but then, I have no idea what his interests are.
I'm glad we don't visit the attic at the same time.
Perhaps if we did
I could find out how he comes and goes.
It *is a* fifteen foot climb.
I will speak to him the next time we meet,
and ask him politely to stay out of the house.
He won't reply,
but sometimes nods in agreement.
A Companion, a Familiar,
but never a Pet

Doug Hile

The Graveyard of Ships

In all of God's heavenly kingdom
    where earthly things are small
age and duty, faith and glory
    stand where others fall.
Yet in this kingdom there is reserved
    a place no mortals dwell
only ships intended for war and fight
    to pass the bowels of hell.
And this kingdom is guarded,
    sure 'tis guarded right,
by eye and beak
    and feather white.
But passing these sentries
    one worries not
for now he enters
    Time Forgot.
Some say when the day
    looses its light
and the steel gray mist
    heralds the night,
the shout of orders,
    it's hard to discern,
a bellow, a curse,
    a "hard astern."
Though few are now left
    to remember those years
when once great hulls
    slipped past gray piers
in this bay of decked warriors,
    aged and hoary,
each hulk low whispers
    its tales of glory.
Their frames were of fir
    bound with gray steel
their bows stiffened concrete
    and courage their keel.
Each ship was a bearer
    of young men of war
destined for battle
    on yon distant shore.
Their bodies were lean
    but of bone stern stuff
and to carry child soldiers
    was task great enough.
The vessels were poor armed,
    exposed with great need,
and what timbers would not
    from torpedo wounds bleed?
Through the Great War's gore
    thunder, gas and shell,
dangers, and blood
    and promise of hell
these wood warriors
    survived far too well.
Now Time takes his toll
    to sound a last knell.
Those once strong beams
    now succumbed to decay
and the powerful steel
    having rusted away
leave only the concrete
    to face the cruel day.
In twilight their courage
    lies imprisoned in slime
their reasons for being
    thought lost for all time.
But where there is death
    life oft springs anew
from a bird dropped seed
    a flower grew.

Donald Grady Shomette

Spring Lettuce

When the March wind tossed sandy Maryland,
when the osprey began to dive for sticks,
when jellyfish floated in, their wombs red,
we planted the first black seeds.

The city was closed, rain lashing
the hospital in tethers of traffic.
Patients played cards, smoked, dreamed.
I stayed late, dictating charts.

Radishes burst first, tearing up to the sun.
Timidly, the lettuce peaked to spy on
the fond farewell of the geese, and duck
at shotgun shells raking from dead blinds.

Many men and women flew in from Europe,
lashed to gurneys, legs twitching,
minds aswarm, families left, souls beaten.
We helped them up, switched their meds.

Time to plant feathery dill and fetid cilantro,
but the purple basil failed of cold.
Starflowers burst through the antique grass.
Tractors flung the furrows wide.

A man pulled a plastic bag over his head and died
in a froth of vomit. We could not revive him.
Police came. Cameras flashed.
Patients cried. I clamped down. Work to do.

White and red radishes fill the fridge.
Time for tomatoes, tamped down with dung.
Tears finally came, as the cages went
around the stalks. How could you suicide in spring?

The inquest ended. No negligence.
Patients found their clothes, called their wives.
Volleyballs pounded the office windows.
A nurse announced. Baby showers.

Now the ospreys tend their eggs
in the locust leaning over the tide.
Underneath the thwocks of croquet balls
we dug the sailboat from the sand.

A woman with AIDS lost her unborn child.
She asked me whether he would go to heaven
or hell, since he was tainted. I replied,
"Heaven, I think." She too wants to die.

A hundred head of lettuce extrude.
Spinach has gone to seed. Girls glide
on the beach. I read Freud.
Black men plant tobacco by hand.

Time for me to leave the ward.
Cocaine addicts revolve through the doors.
I feed the staff lettuce and bread.
Turkey vultures nest in the barn.

Baby jellyfish gather offshore.
Boundaries of ward and garden fade.
Worms swarm in both. I weed and fertilize.
Sails fly, frantically, through the river.

Elspeth Cameron Ritchie

Last Flight

At least *she* perished quickly,
no time for a death song.
Felled by precise surgical swoop,
a flurry of feathers and rose madder
smash against my windowpane.

The accumulation of *his* past
descends into excruciating decay.
Futile medical offensives
yield to detached life support
for the final glide to obliteration.

Simultaneous endings,
synchronous in doom:
A glimpse through the portal
between the panorama of the living
and the flight into eternity.

Whether instant extinction or
bloodless disintegration,
merely a fragile membrane
separates the raptor's talons
from tenacious existence.

Carol Shomette

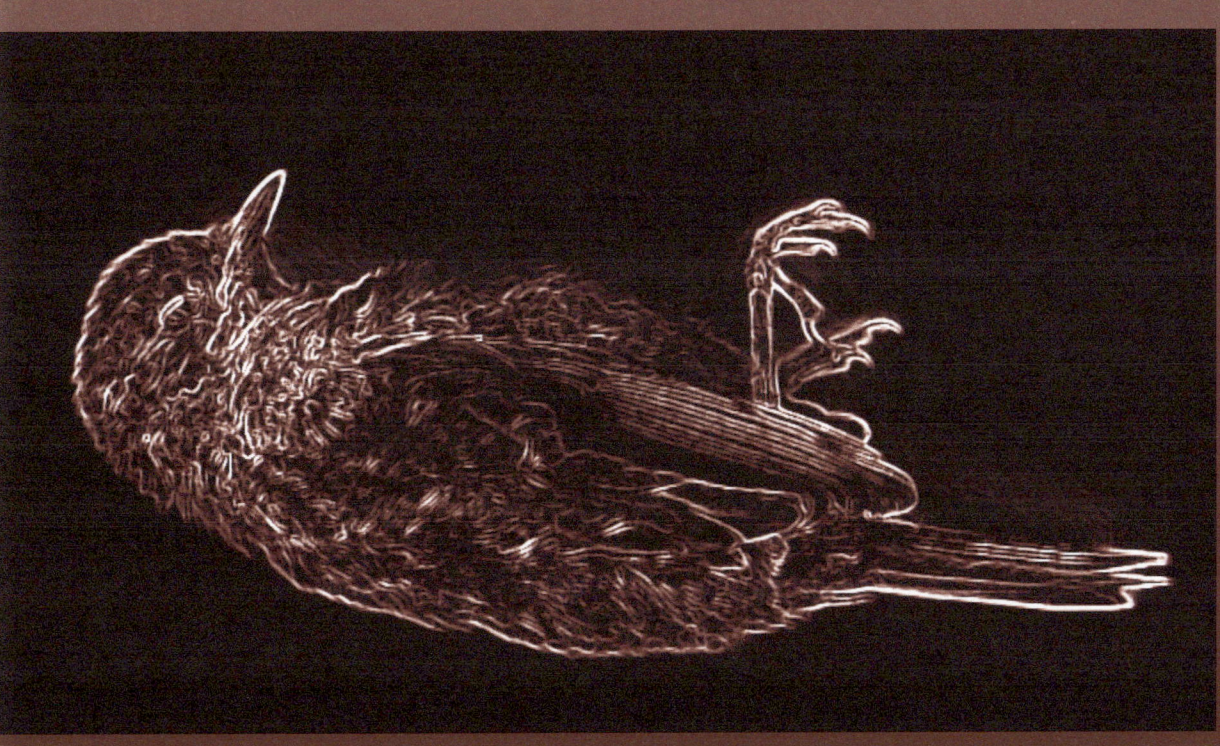

The Crossing

I

The farmhouse was Toni's dream: trumpet vines on the trellis,
a porch and a swing on the palisade above the North Branch,
lavender trim on periwinkle clapboard, a rose-hip door.

Breakfast as the day began: goat cheese on Jewish rye,
coffee on the deck where she sketched the ridge line on her pad,
Haystack Mountain and the Algonquin Heights.

II

Post oaks on the gate road over the bluff onto the bottom,
a rutted lane submerged by sandy eddies at the ford,
the North Branch broad around the bend,
tire tracks at the water's edge.

A kingfisher in the river birch above the crossing,
a hollow rattle, *lie here, lie cold, lie dead, lie still*.

A bitter slog against the wind, I wade across the ford,
an icy visit to the graveyard on the other side.

III

Sunday afternoon, a visit from my sister Claire,
she whispers as she takes my hand, she means no harm:
this place could use a coat of paint.

The periwinkle and the rose-hip fade,
the dream plods on without the dreamer.

George Miller

Audience

The rustling of leaves and water disturbed,
sounds like someone searching, foraging
for something, but voiceless.

Not then two people in a kayak voyaging—

they would talk.

This being moves, but is not concerned
about sounds of disturbance
that may be overheard.

No cat then, or hunting fox,
nor even coyote.

Wouldn't a beaver or woodchuck
mutter to themselves like squirrels do?

But this is a larger fluster
than any of them could fabricate.

I stand still and listen
on this windy peninsula
where few people ever venture.

My ears strain to hear
and my eyes focus with my sense of
the approach of this whoever.

Thrashing among the branches and leaves
down the hillside, black against the water,
a shadow rises into view.

Becomes a great stag—
large with antlers wide spread,
the head held level and neck arched inversely
supporting the weight.

He—no fool—sees me where I stand
and studies me, head moving back and forth
to get my true shape.

He probably can tell I'm not the killing kind—
he approaches for a closer look and stares,
but not for long—you never know—
and so moves on, north now, down into the next ravine,
into the deepest part, where the woods thicken
and the ground turns to marsh beyond,
negotiating low branches—his passage—now silent,
barely disturbing, making no noise.

I follow, but he is gone.

Suzanne Shelden

Seagull Song

It perches near-forgotten on
the curio cabinet shelf,
the porcelain seagull music box,
a birthday gift some years ago.
I haven't touched it, heard it play
in many a mundane month.

Tonight I find my thoughts wound down
and flightless, crumbling into sand.
I'm moved to hold the music box,
hear it sing "By the Beautiful Sea".
Perhaps the song will set the seagull free
in me.

Kate Lassman

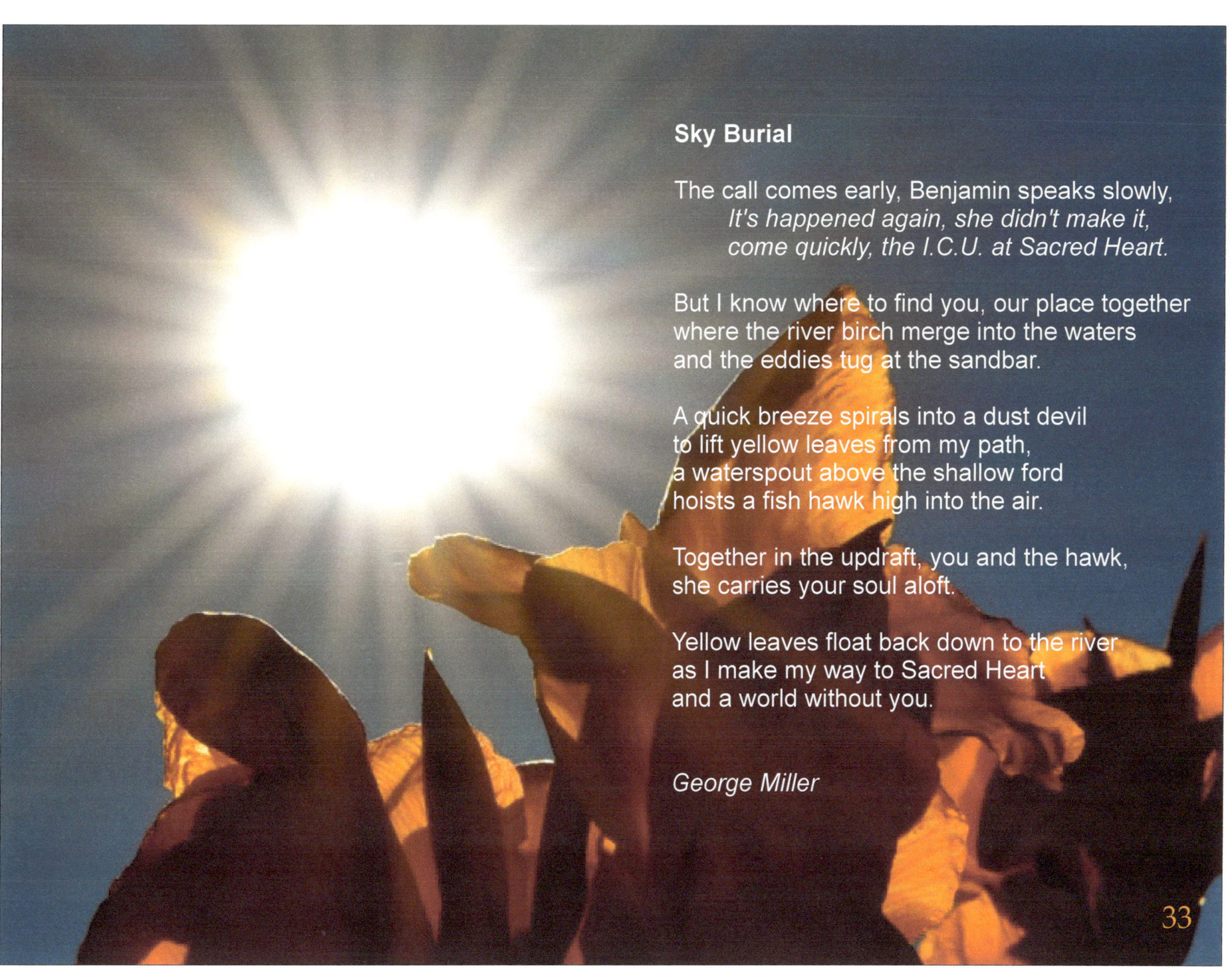

Sky Burial

The call comes early, Benjamin speaks slowly,
   It's happened again, she didn't make it,
   come quickly, the I.C.U. at Sacred Heart.

But I know where to find you, our place together
where the river birch merge into the waters
and the eddies tug at the sandbar.

A quick breeze spirals into a dust devil
to lift yellow leaves from my path,
a waterspout above the shallow ford
hoists a fish hawk high into the air.

Together in the updraft, you and the hawk,
she carries your soul aloft.

Yellow leaves float back down to the river
as I make my way to Sacred Heart
and a world without you.

George Miller

one/sixteenth man

it's as if you're viewing him
through a curved slice of colored opaque glass
it's as if you can only make out…one/sixteenth of him

can't clearly see his face
save from a starboard-side rear angle profile
cardboard legs like the wrong end of a marathon

you can sense his dysfunction
but only…one/sixteenth of it

when he speaks
sounds like salmon swallowing stonehenge
or something
complete gibberish really
because our ears can only interpret
his every /sixteenth syllable

sports an undersized cape, midnight blue
an uppercase "I" over an "/XVI" tattooed on his chest

he's developed x-ray hearing
can always locate his house key and his car key
senses when others are thinking in foreign tongues

hangs his tights at the swamp of serendiptitude
eats black holes for lunch with a side salad
he is the lowest common denominator

he is
one/sixteenth man

Cliff Lynn

Drift

Jeff Smallwood

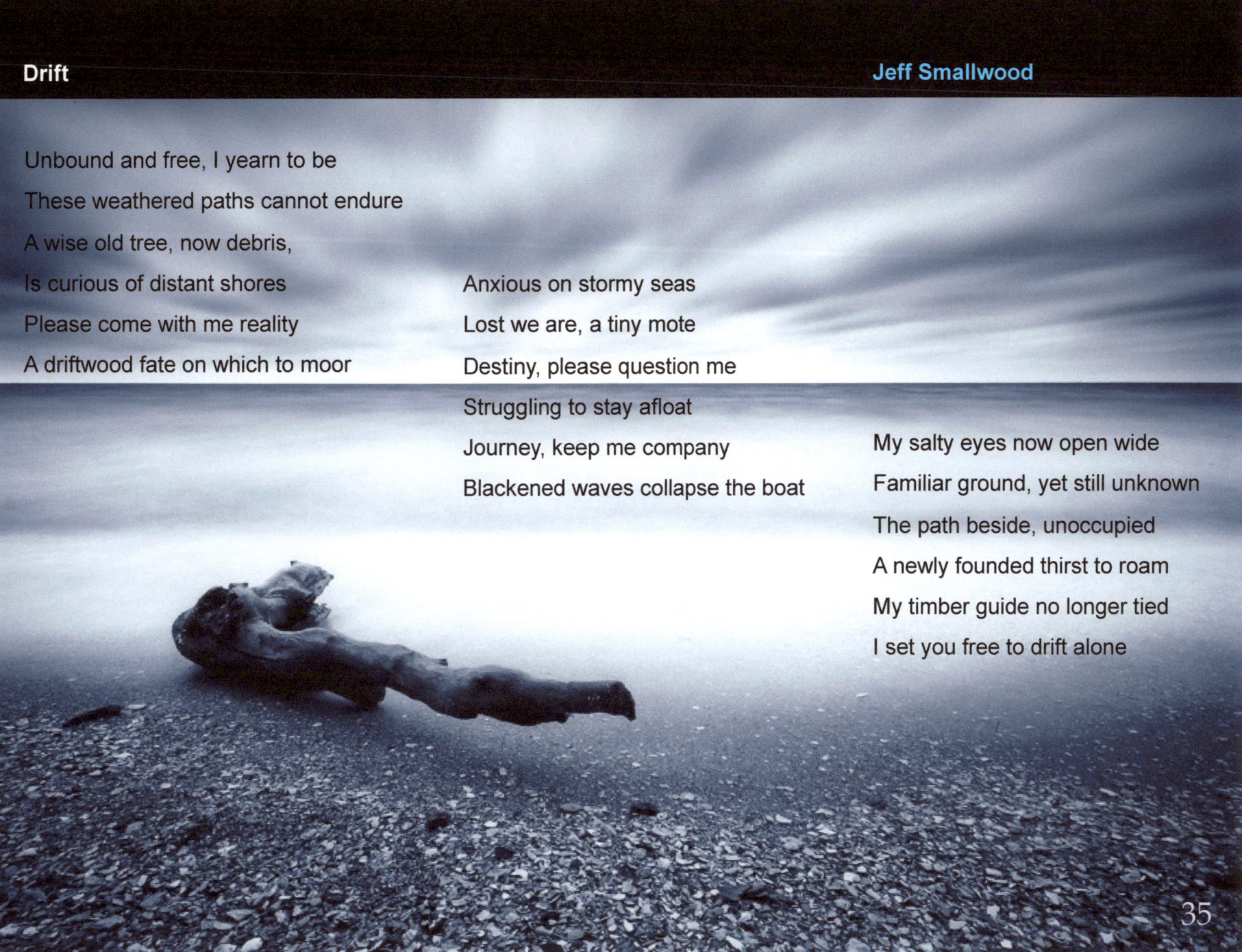

Unbound and free, I yearn to be
These weathered paths cannot endure
A wise old tree, now debris,
Is curious of distant shores
Please come with me reality
A driftwood fate on which to moor

Anxious on stormy seas
Lost we are, a tiny mote
Destiny, please question me
Struggling to stay afloat
Journey, keep me company
Blackened waves collapse the boat

My salty eyes now open wide
Familiar ground, yet still unknown
The path beside, unoccupied
A newly founded thirst to roam
My timber guide no longer tied
I set you free to drift alone

Rocky Jones

Relics You Can Purchase From Me, Discreetly

The jawbone of Sweetpea,
the original Anheuser-Busch Clydesdale

The baby clothes of Pope Francis

Virginia Mayo's ripped stocking

An unripped stocking worn by
Judy Garland and her half sister
at different times

The Sacred Toenail Shaving of Franconio,
patron saint of ditch-dwellers

King Solomon's Unfinished Meat Pie

The preserved amygdala of Caligula

Acknowledgments

Doug Hile: "Used to be Spinnakers," "Blackie,"
 from *Bits & Bytes.*
Rocky Jones: "In This Circle," from the
 online journal *Truck*, February 2016
George Miller: *"Wreck of the Toni Marie,"*
 UP.ST.ART Annapolis, the *Magazine of
 the Annapolis Arts District*, Fall 2016
Kate Lassman: "Hope's Poem," *Connections
 Magazine*, Spring 2019
Cliff Lynn: "rum and rainwater," People's Choice Award,
 2006 Annapolis Bookstore Black Pearl Poetry Contest
Elspeth Cameron Ritchie, "Jewelweed," from Military Medicine 1991,
 "Spring Lettuce," "Jewelweed" from Tearing through the Moon, Poems
 and Prose of an Army Psychiatrist, Wineberry Press 2010
Elspeth Cameron Ritchie, "Notes on the Death of a Deer" from
 Women and Death: 108 American Poets, 1994
Elisavietta Ritchie: *"Sunset, December,"* Reprinted from
 Christian Science Monitor - 1984
Elisavietta Ritchie: "Camille Pissarro Bather Reminisces,"
 The Ledge, Winner of the Poetry Prize, 2012;
 From the Artist's Deathbed; Tiger Upstairs on Connecticut Avenue
Elisavietta Ritchie: "We Wake Beside an Invisible
 River:" *The Broadkill Review, 2017; Prosopisia,
 2017; Harbingers 2017*
Joanne Van Wie; "How to Tell One Man From Another,"
 and "Nights" from *Surfaces, Edges, and Openings.*

Illustrations and Photographs

Donald Grady Shomette, book design, front and back covers,
 pages ii, 1, 6, 7, 9, 11, 13, 16, 17, 18, 20, 22, 23, 25, 26, 27, 28,
 29, 30, 31, 32, 33
Anita Ewing, *Through a Window Brightly*, page 2;
 Call to Prayer, page 4
Camille Pissarro, *The Bather*, page 8
Jeff Smallwood, pages 10, 24, 35
Lester Jay Stone, *Reefing the Jib*, page 15
Amy Fusco, page 12

www.ingramcontent.com/pod-product-compliance
Lightning Source LLC
Chambersburg PA
CBHW042002070526
44584CB00005BA/317